Service Above Self

LIVING A FULFILLED LIFE OF HAPPINESS, LOVE AND INNER PEACE

AJAY GUPTA

Service Above Self: Living a Fulfilled Life of Happiness, Love and Inner Peace

Contents

Foreword by Les Brown

G reetings, my friends. It is an honor to be writing the foreword for this remarkable book, *"Service Above Self: Living a Fulfilled Life of Happiness, Love, and Inner Peace."* The author, Ajay Gupta, has captured a sentiment that is close to my heart: the idea that true fulfillment and joy in life come from serving others without the expectation of anything in return.

As a motivational speaker and author, I have dedicated my life to inspiring people to achieve their full potential and become the best version of themselves. And I have found that the greatest sense of meaning, happiness, and satisfaction in life comes not from what we can get, but from what we can give. When we focus on serving others and using our gifts to make a positive impact in the world, we unlock our consciousness of inner peace, joy, and contentment.

Ajay Gupta is not just the messenger, he is the message. He is the legacy of his father, Anil Gupta, who has been a giver all his life—a person who has impacted and made a difference in other people's lives—and who never asked for anything in return. As the result of his upbringing and inspired by his father, Ajay has also been living a life of contribution—a life of giving to people, of sharing, and of living from a place of love. As we know, God is love, and he who dwelleth in love, dwelleth in God, and God in them. There's a saying, "Judge a man not by what he does, but what he does that he doesn't have to do; and the true quality of a man, is what he does when no one's looking.

Now, because of his experiences and the impact that he himself has made, Ajay wants to encourage others to do what he's done, give, because he knows that his life of giving is not an exception but an example that we can all begin to emulate. In "Service Above Self," Ajay teaches us how to give. His book explores the idea that our lives should be centered around service and impact, rather than the pursuit of personal gain. He emphasizes that our gifts and talents are not meant to be hoarded or used solely for our own benefit, but to be shared and to make your mark on the world with the service you provide.

Throughout the book, Ajay provides practical tools and insights for living a life of service, including tips on finding your unique talents, gifts and passions; overcoming self-doubt, fear, and insecurity; and creating a daily practice of gratitude, reflection, and mindfulness. He also shares inspiring stories of individuals who have dedicated their lives to service and are living lives that matter because of the profound impact they've had in their communities.

As I read through the pages of "Service Above Self," I was struck by how closely the ideas align with my own philosophy on life. I firmly believe that each and every one of us has the power to live a life that matters and to make a positive impact in the world, no matter how small or large our contributions may be. And when we dedicate ourselves to serving others, we unlock a sense of resolve, purpose, and fulfillment that is unmatched. A legendary boxer and humanitarian, once said, "Service to others is the rent you pay for your room here on Earth." And I couldn't agree more with this statement. We are all here for a purpose, and that purpose involves making a positive contribution to the world around us. Whether we realize it or not, we are all connected, and our actions have a ripple effect. You were born and preserved for such a time as this!

In my own life, I have seen the incredible power of service and giving. I have seen how the simple act of helping others can bring immense joy and fulfillment to both the giver and the receiver. And, I have seen how this simple act can lead to incredible feats of greatness.

Service is not just about giving back to others; it is also about unlocking our own potential. When we use our gifts and talents to make a difference, we are tapping into a sense of purpose, passion, and persistence that can help us achieve incredible things. When we are focused on serving others, we are no longer limited by our own fears, doubts, and insecurities; instead, we are empowered to become the best versions of ourselves.

Ajay Gupta's book is a powerful reminder of the transformative power of service and the importance of living a life that will outlive you. It is a call to action for all of us to use our gifts, talents, and skills to help transform the world, and to embrace the true meaning of success—not in what we can accumulate, amass, or achieve—but in what we can give to others.

I highly recommend "Service Above Self" to anyone who is seeking greater satisfaction, joy, and purpose in their lives. This book will inspire you to tap into your unique gifts and talents, and to use them be a positive influence in the world. It is a powerful reminder that when we live a life of service and impact, we unlock the key to true happiness, love, and inner peace. So, let us all take a page out of Ajay Gupta's book and commit to living a life of service and giving.

That's my story, and I'm sticking to it!

Les Brown

To book a Discovery Call with Ajay go to

www.AjayGuptainspires.com/call

Introduction

This book is an opportunity to share stories, occasions, and scenarios that show how acts of pure kindness and gratitude lead to something beautiful. Some of these stories come directly from my own experience; others come from family members or dear friends who know that the secret to living a fulfilled and meaningful life is to live a life of service to others.

It sounds so simple, and it is. Paying it forward means giving something—a smile, your time, some advice—to someone else with no expectations for receiving anything in return; no ulterior motive, you truly want to contribute.

In this book you will read stories from different moments throughout my life, scenarios that taught me lessons, that reinforced my belief in giving unconditionally. (And, at the end of certain chapters, I have included photos to help you connect to the experience even more!) Perhaps reading about these life-changing experiences will inspire you to grow and be more grateful, to give more and pay it forward, and to inspire others to do the same. My friends, my readers, I truly believe the secret to living a joyous, stressless life is merely to contribute to other people and to be grateful for what you have. If every single one of us touches at least one other person's life, if each of us end up positively impacting at least one person's life, then all lives will change.

I didn't write this book to show how great I am, how enlightened, how kind, or to broadcast the amazing things that I've done. In fact, it's just the opposite. My goal in writing this book is to show that I am no different than you are. We all have the opportunity to give; we just have to make that choice! You don't have to give a lot. You don't need to donate thousands of dollars, or to volunteer 40 hours a week. You can make a difference and positively impact someone's life by being kind, looking them in the eye and acknowledging their presence, giving them a hug, listening, or telling a joke! You don't have to wait until your next promotion or pay raise to start giving to others — you can find a way to give now, to start building that muscle in other ways. If you start to build it now, imagine how strong you'll be when you do get that new job or pay raise! It begins with here and now.

I want you to think of showing gratitude and giving unconditionally like they are muscles. If you want to build a muscle and grow stronger than you are today, you don't go to the gym once! You start small…with a 2-pound weight. Then, the next week, you do the same exercise with a 5-pound weight. And before you know it, your muscles are toned and you are curling 45 pounds.

It's the same thing with showing gratitude and giving unconditionally. Start small, and keep doing it to build up the muscle. And before you know it, you're living a life where you choose to be in a state of happiness, contentment, and fulfillment. I'm speaking from experience here because I have been building these "muscles" since I was 9 years old - that's over 20 years! I started slowly and worked my way up gradually. Consistency is the key, my friends. So keep practicing and be determined to keep going.

You should recognize and accept that there will be some days, some weeks, and even some years where you give more than others — and that's okay. It's not a race and you're not in competition! The point is that you keep giving no matter what and whenever you can. I can confidently declare that I am who I am today, and my family is who they are today, because we always put others before ourselves — even in desperate times. I cannot stress enough that giving doesn't have to be financial. Just become aware of serving and making a difference in someone's life. Focus on being kinder and gentler. Smile more, say good morning to people when you see them, ask people how are they really are, give someone a hug, or genuinely compliment them. One compliment could save someone's life.

We should aim to return to a selfless society, family-focused—and not just our biological families, but our communities too. They are also family. Your fellow human beings — even strangers, can make up a universal family.

So how does this all start? Great question! And there's an easy answer: it starts with you! So, dear reader, I invite you to join me on this beautiful journey. It is my greatest wish that this book inspires you to grow and contribute more because together, we can make a difference, one person at a time!

Before we begin, I would like to take the opportunity to acknowledge certain people in my life who have helped this book become a reality.

Acknowledgements

My dad, Anil Gupta, and my mum, Meena Gupta, for being the most supportive and loving parents a person could ever hope for. You continue to inspire me by embodying the principles outlined in this book. Thank you for consistently showing me unconditional love and providing our family with the support we need to make the difference we're each here to make.

My sister, Anu Gupta, life wouldn't be the same without you, I am so proud of who you are and your light and presence inspires me to continue my mission to serve and inspire.

My grandparents, Sushil and Shanti Gupta, Krishan and Bimla Goyal, all of whom have played an integral role in the love I have for myself, my family, and our culture. Thank you for sacrificing your lives for all of us.

All of my cousins and extended family members, who are like my siblings. You have all showed unconditional love and support over the years.

Thank you, Mimi Loftus, for helping me to create this book by translating the incredible experiences I've had into beautifully written stories.

Lastly, to all of my mentors who have supported me during my journey, the ones who taught me what to do, and what not to do. I am grateful for all the lessons along the way.

Chapter 1:

A Boy Named Ajay

In April 2019, I flew to India after receiving a very last minute invitation to meet His Holiness the Dalai Lama in his home in Dharamshala, India. The invite arrived while I was recovering from pneumonia and a lung infection, but I knew I could not pass on the opportunity. So, three weeks after being hospitalized, I flew to India. Ironically, the day I landed in India, I read a headline: *His Holiness Dalai Lama hospitalized in Delhi.*

Sadly, due to his illness, I didn't get the chance to meet him. And, as honored as I was to meet His Holiness, I knew this trip was going to be magical because I had planned to remain in the country for a month to volunteer and visit different non profit organizations. Before the trip, I reached out to friends for suggestions about organizations or charities in India where I could volunteer. Some friends recommended a few charities in Rishikesh, and so that's where I started.

You may recognize Rishikesh as the holy city that rests on the foothills of the Himalayas where The Beatles studied transcendental meditation, but it has long been and continues to be a Hindu pilgrimage site. With its heightened spiritual energy and people known for their appreciation of the sacred river Ganges, Rishikesh was the perfect starting point for my month in India.

I was greeted by a kind driver at the Dehradun Airport, and we drove 40 minutes to the city. When we arrived, the driver parked the car next to a bustling riverbank and told me we would have to take a boat from here. I had no idea where I was, but I remember thinking how cool it was to go from Delhi to Dehradun on a plane, get a taxi from the airport to the river, and then a boat to the *ashram*[1], Parmarth Niketan. This ashram is well-known and host to the International Yoga Festival every year.

Upon arrival, I went directly to the evening *puja*[2]. It was truly one of the most beautiful experiences I have ever witnessed — a *puja aarti*[3] on the side of Mother Ganga. It was so powerful that I could feel the energy spreading through every inch of my body, and I had the honor of participating in the evening *Ganga Aarti*[4] each night I stayed at the ashram.

---

[1] A spiritual sanctuary
[2] Sanskrit for worship
[3] A devotional ritual that uses fire as an offering while singing devotional songs and chanting prayers
[4] The Hindu religious ritual performed nightly at sunset on the banks of the Ganges (known as the "mother")

At the ashram were some of the most peaceful, centered, calming people I have ever met. Each one was so present and each one had a warming energy that helped me to be even more present, even more loving. That's what happens when you surround yourself with beautiful souls!

There was this one man in particular with such a beautiful heart and soul; he had this gentle yet dynamic energy surrounding and emanating from him. He spoke about giving unconditionally, and I was fascinated by how closely we aligned in our thinking! I felt I could learn from him, and so I accepted the invitation to join some people for dinner following a *satsang*⁵ hosted by Sadhvi Ji, a beautiful soul and spiritual leader who has dedicated her life to serving others at the Parmarth Niketan ashram since 1997. Curious as to who this amazing man was, I checked his Instagram profile and realized we shared the same passion and desire to make a difference in people's lives. I also noticed he had millions of followers. Millions!

But who was this person? I noticed that when people approached him, they either shook his hand or hugged him, and he treated each person as if they were the only one in the world. He really listened and honored them. And so, I felt inspired to introduce myself, and that's when I realized he was Prince EA! Imagine that — this man can fill a stadium, has billions of views on YouTube, and speaks to audiences of thousands, but he treated everyone as an equal; he not

---

⁵ A gathering of like-minded, uplifting people, especially on a spiritual path

only spoke about giving unconditionally, but his actions matched his words. We shared a beautiful conversation, and we continued to joke and laugh throughout the evening.

It was such an amazing, memorable night that taught me how important it is to be fully present and to appreciate every opportunity life offers. When we live in the frequency of Giving and Loving unconditionally, that's what we attract. Surround yourself with people who understand and practice this principle, and it will reinforce the truth.

As I mentioned, I had reached out to several people for ideas and suggestions of places where I could be of service. While I was in Rishikesh, a good friend told me about an orphanage in the hilltops, home to more than 50 children. She urged me to visit, saying they would love to have me as a speaker, and that I would love the experience of being able to connect with precious children. I called the next day and connected with Gagan, the orphanage manager, to settle on a day and time when I would visit. I felt so honored for the opportunity to be of service.

The night before I was scheduled to speak, I called to confirm with the director of the orphanage.

"Yes!" he replied. "We are all good for tomorrow. We are so excited to meet you!"

The morning came quickly, and I woke up bright and early, excited to start my day and visit the orphanage. Just down the street from the ashram was a *chaiwallah*[6] who made the most incredible masala chai, so incredible that I would visit him three or four times a day! That morning, I left the ashram and headed to get my morning chai. What a great start to what was sure to be a fantastic day!

Even though it was about 100 degrees Fahrenheit, I felt like challenging myself by doing something different, so I decided to walk to the orphanage instead of getting transport. By all means, I could have taken a *Tuk-Tuk*[7] for $1, but my heart told me that I should hike it for the adventure. I was going to be sweaty when I reached the top of the hill, but I was in India, so it was the perfect place and time to push myself in unfamiliar ways. Of course, since I was going to be presenting and speaking to a group of children and their caretakers, I made sure to leave in time to dry off and grab some food.

The journey to the orphanage was long and hilly, but making this difficult walk was important to me. As I walked up the side of the mountain, countless vehicles passed me. Smoke filled my lungs as tractors, motorbikes, cars, and scooters whizzed past at high speed. Plus, the heat was scorching, making me sweat profusely and I was dripping wet. I could have signaled for a Tuk-Tuk or scooter that passed by for a lift, but I didn't. I have two strong legs that I am so grateful for! I wanted to experience the walk, especially since walking is the only form of transportation for so many people in India.

---

[6] A man who makes tea; an integral part of Indian culture
[7] A taxi

I urge you to challenge yourself — put yourself in those uncomfortable situations. The more comfortable you can get being uncomfortable, the stronger and more resilient you become as a human.

Once I reached the top, I felt amazing because I pushed through the discomfort. Plus, the view of Rishikesh was stunning! I stopped at a cafe to drink some water and cool down. Once I felt ready again, I headed to the orphanage.

When I walked through the main door, I immediately caught a whiff of animal dung. Looking to my right, I spotted a pig's sty, and on the other side of the pigs were chickens. That's India!

There was no sign of children so I walked through the building until I saw someone. I asked for Gagan, the manager whom I spoke with the night before to confirm for the visit. After a pause, she said, "Gagan not here." She then pointed me down a hallway, and so I followed her direction. As I walked, looking for someone who could help me, I spent some time taking it all in. It didn't smell good, and it was really run down.

After a while, I found another member of staff. "Sir, I am looking for Gagan." He didn't say a word but pointed me in another direction.

At this point, I was growing really frustrated. There was no sign of any children, the heat was almost unbearable, and the stench was getting to me. Nevertheless, I continued in the direction the gentleman pointed and found a woman washing dishes in the kitchen.

I walked in and asked for Gagan for the third time. She said, "They have gone to the beach on a field trip." I said, "But I was scheduled to speak with them."

She just smiled and repeated the same words. "They have gone to the beach."

I was furious! I thought, *What does she mean they took a field trip? We scheduled this talk for today and I confirmed with the guy last night! I prepared a presentation especially for these children. I WALKED up that hill, pushed myself, and now no one is here? They're at the beach?!?*

That's when I snapped myself out of that type of thinking. I reminded myself that "When you're in your head, you're dead!" So, I shifted my mindset and decided that there was a reason this happened, but I didn't know what it was yet. As soon as I changed my thinking about the situation, I was immediately calm and ready for whatever was to come.

I couldn't stay angry. It's India, and I love my India. Perhaps I would get another opportunity to speak to those kids, so I took my leave. I waved goodbye to the staff members I had spoken to and left the orphanage.

As I walked out of the main doors, I turned toward the center of town. That's when I noticed a little child walking in the same direction just beside me; he was a happy young kid, and started talking to me with enthusiasm and poise.

"Hello! How are you today?"

I replied, "I'm doing great! How are you?"

"I am also doing great! Where are you going?"

"I just came from the orphanage and now I'm heading back down to *Ram Jhula*[8] Bridge. Where are you going?" "I am going to the store up ahead."

As I paid more attention to him, I noticed he had such joy in his step and his energy was infectious. He was only 7 years old, but he was so confident and comfortable talking with a complete stranger! Plus, his spoken English was excellent. It was uncommon to meet someone in this area who spoke English at all, and here was a child who spoke fluently and with ease.

"What is your name?" I asked him.

"Ajay," he replied.

---

[8] A narrow suspension footbridge that spans 750 feet across the Ganges

I stopped in my tracks and that made him stop, too. I high fived him, saying, "You'll never believe this! My name is also Ajay and I am 28."

He grinned and said, "Ajay, you have a cool name. And you're four times older than I am!"

"Oh, so you're good at math, too, huh?"

I was amazed. This kid was awesome! And I never would have met him if the children at the orphanage hadn't gone to the beach. THIS was why I made this journey — to meet Ajay! I had a moment of gratitude and acknowledged how life was always happening for me.

We arrived at the local convenience store and Ajay handed the shopkeeper a 10 rupee note, and in exchange, he was given two bags of chips. He explained to me that one was for him, and the other was for his younger sister.

I asked if I could walk back to Ajay's home because we were having a lovely conversation. I was so impressed with how this young boy carried himself. He radiated confidence, had a great sense of humor, was kind and thoughtful, and highly intelligent.

When we reached his gate, I helped him open the latch and then his father came out of the house.

I said, "*Uncle*[9], are you Ajay's dad?" "Yes."

"Uncle, my name is Ajay, too. You have an incredibly gifted son. It was an honor to meet him, and to meet you, too." Ajay's father beamed, clearly proud of his son.

After a brief conversation, I waved as I bid them goodbye and left their yard. I was so moved and inspired by this young boy, that I had a desire to do something for him.

I walked back into the center of town and the local convenience store. I asked the shopkeeper, "How often does Ajay come to his store?"

"Sir, he comes once a week, always with 10 rupees, and he buys two bags of chips—one for him and one for his sister, and they're the same brand."

I said, "Uncle, I want to buy every bag of his favorite chips." He looked at me, confused. "All of them?"

"All of them."

Of course, the shopkeeper could not understand my experience with Ajay, and I didn't have the ability to explain the concept of paying it forward and the power of giving unconditionally in Hindi! Together, we filled two large plastic with all of the chips Ajay loved, about 60 in total.

---

[9] A term of endearment and respect for men in India

I paid him him 500 rupees (about $6) and headed back to Ajay's house, receiving stares from people who must have wondered what this guy was doing carrying two huge bags filled with chips. When I arrived, I entered their property and had intended just to drop the bags and leave. But when Ajay's father realized what was in the bags, he asked me how his children were going to eat so many bags of chips. Ajay came bounding into the room, with a smile that seemed to melt his father's heart.

"*Thik hai, papa*[10]! We can share with the kids across the street!" He was, of course, referring to the children who lived in the orphanage, the ones I never got to meet. And in that moment, I realized how everything happens for a reason. What were the chances that I would run into Ajay at the exact time I did? If I had taken a Tuk-Tuk that morning instead of walking, or if the orphans hadn't spontaneously taken a field trip, I wouldn't have met him.

I was so impressed by Ajay's attitude and the way he handled himself! Here was this child with practically nothing—but he had so much joy in his heart that it humbled me. Buying the chips was a small act of kindness, and the least I could have done to honor such a young gentleman. And what a beautiful turn of events to learn he wasn't keeping his good fortune only for himself. He was already practicing service above self.

---

[10] "It's OK, dad!" in Hindi

You never know the impact you can make in someone's life. If you can help someone change their focus or change the meaning for something in their life, it can open up a world of possibilities.

Show Up. Always say YES! When things don't go your way, what are you going to do about it? If you can't change the situation, then change your thinking about the situation. I was able to push my body, and I am grateful for my strength. Admittedly, I was frustrated and annoyed when I first learned about the beach trip, but as soon as I changed the meaning about that situation, I was able to open myself to the gift that came from it: meeting Ajay.

I was never able to return to the orphanage, but over the next month, I spoke at different organizations and helped to feed families and children along the way. This trip started with the promise of meeting His Holiness the Dalai Lama, but his health prevented that from happening. I could have taken that turn of events as an omen or allowed the disappointment to infect my mindset. But thanks to years of practicing gratitude and knowing that life is happening for me, I was able to embrace the change and experience beautiful and magical moments that I would have otherwise missed.

Chaiwallah Uncleji in action. Notice the respect he has for his space.

The final product! Now you understand why I came here 5 times a day!

Thank you for showing me how important it is to pour all your love into whatever you do!

Chapter 2:

The Gift of Losing Everything

In September 2012, Sage Robbins, Tony Robbins' wife, invited me to work with Robbins Research International (RRI). I had no idea what I was going to be doing but I knew it would be a chance for me to grow, contribute, and make a difference in people's lives. How could I resist? Plus, it's really difficult to say no to Sage Robbins! She is one of the most loving, generous, selfless people I have ever met; in her core, she understands and lives the ideals of Service Above Self. So, if Sage asks something of you, you say yes! I am forever grateful to her for recognizing something in me that I didn't even realize was there.

As part of my role with RRI, I traveled a lot. Every four or five months, I would re-locate to another major city in the US. In the four years I spent traveling and speaking with Tony, I had the privilege of living in Miami, Tampa, Austin, New York, San Diego, Los Angeles, San Fransisco, and Chicago.

In and around those cities, I would drive from workshop to workshop, which meant I spent more time in my car than in my apartment! I always made it a point to carry a case of water bottles, as well as apples and bananas to give to homeless people at traffic stops or gas stations. I encourage you to consider doing the same, because it's a relatively easy way to set yourself up to give unconditionally and to be of service to people who are not as fortunate.

In 2013, I was living in Tampa, Florida. It was Christmas, and most of my friends had already traveled home for the holidays. Since my family's home is only an hour's drive from Tampa, I found myself in the unique position of being alone and having solitude. What a gift! I decided to use some of my time on self-care because I have learned how important it is to treat myself with the same respect and kindness that I give to others. Remember, self-care isn't selfish; it's self-less. It was during my gratitude exercise that an idea came to me: I could assemble and deliver bags of food and water to the homeless people in downtown Tampa. So, I posted on Facebook, asking friends and family to join me and distribute the bags the next day. I was filled with joy!

I woke up very bright and early the next morning and followed my usual routine. I started with my gratitude exercise, I journaled, and then I went for a run before logging onto my Facebook account. The post received over 100 "likes!" YES!!! I got so excited about the prospect of a whole group of us giving our time to connect with some people who are too often overlooked. Then I started reading through the comments to see who would be joining me.

"That's awesome!"

"Namaste."

"Wish I could help!"

The post had 100 "likes" and about 50 comments, but not one person offered to join me or contribute to the event. At first, I was really upset. To be honest, I was furious because I felt disappointed and let down. I had set an expectation for others to just drop everything and give up their time, and when that didn't happen, I took it personally. This is the danger of having an expectation and then creating a story and meaning without taking into consideration all the facts. But, thanks to years of practicing the "self-awareness muscle," I don't stay upset for very long. I spend time experiencing the emotion before giving myself time to get over it. I ask myself a series of questions, which I answer truthfully and without emotion or ego.

What is the truth?	The truth was I only gave people 10 hours to commit.
Why am I feeling upset?	I was feeling upset because I was focusing on myself and what I thought was missing.
What really happened?	What happened was that the people I reached out to couldn't commit on such short notice.
Did I jump to conclusions?	Absolutely! I made up all kinds of stories as to why no one "wanted" to join me.
What can I choose to focus on right now?	I chose to focus on the difference I was about to make.
When would be a good time to let go?	Now! (p.s. The answer is always "Now!")

Sometimes, I need to give myself time to process what I'm feeling and to examine the meaning I'm attaching to it. But then, I can let it go and move on.

That morning, I closed my laptop, did some deep breathing followed by 10 jumping jacks, and I was ready to go! I gave thanks for my heart, for my hands, my eyes, my strong legs, for the precious life I had been given, and for my ability to be of service.

You should have seen how quickly a smile returned to my face! I didn't know the reasons why people did not offer to join me, but it didn't matter—I would do it on my own.

And so, I went to Walmart and purchased non-perishable food, water, and personal hygiene items. As I was putting the bags into the trunk of my car, I realized that I did need some help. I called a dear friend of mine, Tom, who was also a speaker with Tony Robbins.

"Hey, Ajay! How are you?" Tom beamed when he answered the call.

"Tom, brother. I am fantastic. But I need your help. I have bags and bags of food and water, and I need some assistance in delivering them to people downtown."

"Just tell me where to meet you, and I'll be there in an hour." In the time it took Tom to reach my apartment, I had assembled about 50 brown bags and loaded them into my car. Together, we headed downtown, both very excited to be of assistance to people in need. We drove past a park where we saw a makeshift tent city. That would be our first stop. We distributed bags to 20 or so men and women, and took the time to talk to some of them. We then jumped back in the car and drove to another area of town, searching for more people we could help. At a red traffic light, a police cruiser pulled up next to us. I rolled down my window to get the officer's attention. The officer rolled down his window and so I introduced ourselves. "Good morning, officer. My name is Ajay Gupta and this is my brother from another mother, Tom."

The officer smiled at that, and I continued. "We have bags of food and hygiene items to distribute to homeless men and women in the area. Can you please direct us where we can find people to serve?"

The officer actually got out of his car and walked to my window. He reached his hand in to shake mine, saying, "Thank you for what y'all are doing."

"No officer, thank *you* for everything *you* do," I replied. "Every day, you risk your life to protect us; every day, your children risk losing their father, your wife risks losing her husband. Thank you for protecting us selflessly."

He nodded his acknowledgement and said, "If you head along this road and turn right, you will see benches with people who may need help. Then continue straight and after about a mile you will find a church. I guarantee you, there will be people you can support and help there."

We thanked him and headed toward the Church. I parked the car and we saw a man sitting on the stairs of the Church. Tom and I approached and asked if he needed food and water. He wasn't hungry, but he did want water. I handed him a couple of bottles of water and started to walk away when I heard Tom ask, "Why are you homeless? What's your story?"

I was a little surprised at the bluntness of Tom's question. But I knew he asked from a place of love and compassion, because that was always Tom's motivation. Although I had spent time talking casually to some of the men and women we met, it had never occurred to me to ask why they were living on the street.

We learned that Randy had lived in Florida all his life. He had been married with children, and he and his wife ran a small business that brought in more than $100,000 a year. Since their business was thriving, he didn't pay much attention to the details because his wife handled the operations while he focused on sales, client satisfaction, and generating new business.

After years of marital problems, his wife divorced him and left him with nothing. She took their children, their house, and even their business. She had put everything in her name, and so Randy didn't have claim to anything they had built together.

Randy found work but he had to start from scratch since he didn't even have access to the bank account he had shared with his wife. He struggled to find a place to live, which caused him a lot of anxiety and stress. His situation became dire when he lost his job. That's how he ended up living on the streets.

One morning, one of Randy's friends invited him to have breakfast at a local McDonalds. At the end of their meal, he went to use the restroom. He was approached by a member of staff who denied him access, saying, "This restroom is for paying customers only."

Randy replied, "I am a paying customer. My friend purchased this meal for us."

The employee replied, "No. You smell. You are homeless. And you can't use this restroom."

The argument escalated until it got physical. There was pushing and shoving from both parties until Randy pulled out a knife and stabbed the employee in the arm. Paramedics rushed to the restaurant while the police rushed Randy to jail.

He was convicted of assault with a deadly weapon and served a prison sentence. When he was released, with nowhere to go, he returned to living on the streets.

Months later, Randy was sitting on a park bench when he was approached by another homeless man. They started to argue, and it got physical. Ironically, the other man stabbed Randy in the back. He was taken by ambulance to the hospital, where he had surgery to heal the stab. It took him several months to recover, and he still feels extreme pain from the wound. In fact, Randy cannot raise his arm past a certain point because of the damage to the muscle in his back.

A year after Randy was stabbed, he was invited to this Church where he found peace and a sense of gratitude. It was also where he learned how to forgive. Because he understands the power of gratitude and of giving, he serves food at this Church every day to other homeless men and women.

One day while Randy was serving food, he noticed a man standing in line waiting to be served. When the man was in front of Randy, he asked, "Do you not know who I am?"

"Yes," replied Randy as he ladled some food on the man's plate. "I know who you are."

"Don't you want to kill me?" the man asked with pain in his eyes.

Randy smiled gently at the man in front of him, the same man who had stabbed him over a year ago.

"No, friend. I don't want to kill you. I forgive you." The man standing in front of Randy started to cry and said simply, "Thank you."

After he finished sharing, I asked, "Randy, I appreciate your story and it was so moving. May I ask a favor?"

Randy looked surprised. "Of course. Anything."

"I am 22 years old and my brother Tom here is 37. What is one piece of advice you could give us before we leave?" Randy replied without hesitation, almost as if he knew what we were going to ask and had already prepared an answer. "Monday through Friday I sit on the steps of this church. I see people running and walking up and down the street, some with their headphones in, some on their phones. Most don't pay attention to what's around them, and no one stops to appreciate anything. Look at this beautiful church! Look at the architecture! It's magnificent! But no one sees it. No one ever looks up at the beautiful sky, or listens to the wind rustle through the trees. Life goes by like this," he snapped his fingers. "And trust me, you never know when things are going to change for you just like this." Again, he snapped his fingers.

"As crazy as this sounds," he continued, "I know that everything that happened to me in my life is a gift. Losing everything, going to jail, being on the streets - all of it."

Randy got a little emotional, and held up his finger for us to give him a second. He swallowed back his tears and continued. "I had everything society told me I needed: a big house, 2 cars, closets full of clothes and shoes. Everything. But I was never happy. I was always angry and frustrated because all I noticed was what wasn't there. All I did was compare myself to other people. One time, my neighbor came home with a new car and I was so pissed off. I remember thinking, *That guy down the street has it made. His life is perfect.* I wonder how many people thought that about me."

Randy paused, took a deep breath, and looked up at the sky, smiling before continuing.

"Ajay, I know I got long-winded to answer your question, but my advice to you is this: Appreciate everything around you. And I don't mean just the stuff. Appreciate this friendship you have" he said nodding toward Tom. "Appreciate the clean air you breathe, your strong legs, your sense of humor! If you look for what's missing, that's all you'll see."

He stood up and extended his hand to us. "Now, if you'll excuse me, I am expected in the kitchen. We're cooking beef stew today and it's a fan favorite!" And with a big smile, Randy made his way back into the church where he would serve every man, woman, and child who came for a meal before returning to the shelter where he stayed these days.

Randy's lesson reminded me of a piece of art hanging in my bedroom. It says:

Yesterday is history.

Tomorrow is a mystery.

Today is a gift,

That's why we call it the present.

My friends, today is a gift; you are a gift. Life goes by so quickly, so you must appreciate everything and everyone around you. Recognize and be grateful that you live in a city that's protected by men and women who risk their lives every day to keep us safe. Be grateful that you live in a country where you aren't worried when the next bomb is going to come crashing down on you. Be grateful you have clean water and electricity. Be grateful! For when you are grateful, fear and anxiety disappear.

That day, I learned an important lesson. When I handed Randy the bottle of water, he was just some homeless man. I figured maybe he had used drugs, or came from a horrible home life. What a dangerous assumption I had made.

Everyone - no matter who it is, has a story to tell. We each go through our own experiences in life and that's what makes our life so unique to us. Speak to people, ask them questions, get to know them and see what lessons they can teach you. There is a lesson in everything, we have to ask or seek it to find it.

It's not what happens in life, it's who you become. Situations will come up, but how you handle them is what defines you. When Randy learned to forgive, it gave him freedom. Freedom from anger, freedom from resentment, freedom from the need for revenge. Randy has peace in his heart, because forgiveness is the express pathway to freedom.

Randy and myself in Tampa.

Chapter 3:

Generating Love and Light

Reflecting on my travels, I find myself in awe as I think about the people I have had the honor to meet and spend time with. They have such incredibly difficult lives filled with uncertainty, constant struggle, and hardships that most people can't imagine. And yet, they are some of the kindest, most loving, selfless, and generous people I know. This chapter highlights two such individuals whom I met in 2019 and who continue to impact my life to this day.

In 2019, I made a trip to visit His Holiness the Dalai Lama (HHDL) where I was introduced to a remarkable young man, Kailash Bhaiya. In Hindi, *Bhaiya* means "brother," and I felt grateful and honored to call Kailash brother since this man truly is a gift from God.

Since 2015, Kailash has served as official Hindi interpreter for HHDL, and he does this job without pay. He commits to this time-consuming and demanding work without earning any money because he was called to do so, and he understands that the principle of giving unconditionally is the secret to living a fulfilled life of peace and happiness.

Kailash was raised in Nagla Dhaukal, a tiny village located in the Mainpuri district, a rural part of India. This village is so small they do not have cell service or even electricity. Children do not go to school; they are resigned to lives of extreme hardship, knowing they will simply continue in the same way the villagers have existed for hundreds of years. There, Kailash, along with his ten siblings, farmed the land and raised livestock with little thought of a life other than the one he had.

But then, one of his older brothers, Suresh, made it out of the village all the way to Nalanda University, and that opportunity opened doors not only for Suresh, but for Kailash, as well. Thanks to his brother's example, Kailash realized that education was the key—if he was going to help create a better life for the children of his village, they were going to need a school.

In the early 2000s, Kailash and his family committed to building a school where village children could live and study Maths, English, and Writing among other subjects. But how could this family from an impoverished village build a school? For 15 years, they slowly raised money and gradually built the school; they never gave up, and they never focused on what they didn't have. Rather, they simply moved forward, sacrificing their own time, energy, sleep, and other precious resources. It took 15 years to raise enough money to build a school where 15 children share one toilet without a lid; where 4 children sleep together in one single bed; where tattered curtains substituted for actual doors.

The school (Youth Buddhist Society) is in Sankisa, a town about 5 miles from Nagla Dhaukal. Without it, the children from the village wouldn't have any education because children of rural farmers just become farmers themselves. No one thinks beyond what they know, and no one believes they can do better than what they have.

While I was in Sankisa, I visited the school and that experience reinforced the importance of community and of giving unconditionally. As I prepared for the visit, I thought of ways I could contribute and provide some assistance, but I wanted it to be fun and special for the children. So, I purchased and assembled "goody bags" filled with personal hygiene items, school supplies, toys, and of course, chocolate and other sweets.

When the children opened their bags, they started jumping up and down because it's rare that they are given anything, much less a special package just for them. They were so grateful and filled with joy — showing each other their items, giggling and playing with their toys and enjoying the delicious candy. And then there was a moment that I will never forget.

I was standing with Kailash, discussing the ways he wanted to grow and improve the school when a little boy came up to me. I bent down to be eye-to-eye with him and he held out his hand. In it was a piece of candy from his bag.

"For you," he said.

I smiled at the child and replied, "Thank you, but that candy is for you!"

"But you don't have any," he insisted, and continued to hold out his hand.

I was so touched that I started to cry. Here was a child who had literally nothing other than his basic needs met, and when he received something special, his inclination was to share it. Again, I politely declined. "It's ok. You enjoy it."

That's when I saw his body language completely change. When he approached me, he stood tall with his head high and a bright smile on his face. But now his shoulders shrunk a little and he dropped his gaze. In that moment, I realized I had taken some of his joy by not accepting his offer.

"On second thought, I would love that piece of candy." His smile returned and he put the candy in my hand. I hugged him and thanked him, and he trotted back to join the other boys from his school.

What a lesson! That little child taught me that giving unconditionally is not one- sided, and that I needed to learn how to receive graciously.

Over 20 years ago, Kailash and his family decided that the children of his village matter. But despite working constantly to raise money and find donations, they had made minimal progress over the years. The conditions were dire, and I asked what they needed to elevate the school from dirt floors and plywood beds to the kind of environment where real learning could happen.

"Oh, brother," Kailash replied, his eyes darting around the space, almost as if he were calculating the sum so far out of his reach. "We are talking thousands of dollars. It takes us a year to raise the funds needed for simple repairs. We designed the garden to grow enough food to feed the children and even have some left over to sell, and we also sell the cow dung that people use as fuel, but it's not enough to make the kind of improvements you are talking about."

I had recently read that on average, Americans spend $1500-$2500 annually on designer coffee, the amount that Kailash needed for beds, concrete floors, working toilets, and doors. For the $1500 I spent on coffee last year, we could build enough beds so that each child could have his own, plus have enough for the additional construction we discussed. I pledged to Kailash that I would find the money and we would make his vision come true.

As we wrapped up the tour of the school and started walking out of the yard, I mentioned making arrangements to stay in a hotel nearby.

Kailash stopped abruptly. "Brother, no! You will take my room. I can sleep in the little office over there."

I followed his finger that pointed to the "office," a closet sized space with a simple chair and table.

"You'll sleep where?" I looked around the tiny room for something that resembled a bed.

"We have a little mat. It's quite comfortable, really!" A mat. On the floor.

Although they have "nothing" as people in the west tend to define it, his parents and grandparents instilled strong beliefs about what's really important in life, similar to "Service Above Self."

You see, when you adopt an attitude of gratitude and a belief in giving unconditionally, you start to attract like-minded people. Meeting Kailash Bhaiya and his family strengthened my commitment to serve others. If they could dedicate their lives to acts of service from a place of pure love, then I certainly could!

I am happy to share that we raised the funds they needed to build enough beds to accommodate all of the children, poured concrete floors, plastered and painted the walls, replaced the curtains with doors and windows, and installed proper bathrooms with working toilets with seats. However, there is still much to be done. Therefore, proceeds from the sale of this book will go to this school and others, and so you are already part of the solution!

For the first time in their lives, the children of the village have hope because Kailash and his family believed in them. Affording the village children an education— one that so many people take for granted—gives them an opportunity to do something greater for themselves, to leave their village and find meaningful work in a larger city, which then allows them to support their families.

But the reach of Kailash Bhaiya does not end in Sankisa or with the small village school he helped create. As the official Hindi interpreter for His Holiness Dalai Lama, Kailash was able to introduce his niece Aastha and nephew Ankit to the Tibetan Cultural Village School in Dharamshala. The school is primarily sponsored by HHDL with some donations, but it is not enough to properly manage and run the school. As is the case with many non-profit organizations, they are always seeking support.

On the heels of my visit to Sankisa, I made my way to Dharamshala where Kailash arranged for Aastha and Ankit to give me a tour of their school. There I met the Head Mother of one of the the girls' residence hall, Ama La, who is responsible for the care and well-being of the 45 girls who live in that particular residence. The name "Ama La" translates to "mother," and that is who she is.

Ama La came to the Village School in the early 1970s when she was 22 years old. She willingly gave up her personal freedom to spend her life in service to His Holiness the Dalai Lama and the female students at the school. For more than 50 years, Ama La has started her day at 5:00AM. She prepares breakfast for the girls (and later lunch and dinner), makes sure they are all dressed in uniform and ready for their classes.

While the girls are in class, Ama La straightens their rooms, cleans the residence hall, makes arrangements for repairs, and handles all the unforeseen issues that arise every day. In addition to her custodial duties, Ama La is responsible for making sure the girls study every evening and on weekends, and are prepared for their lessons and exams. She supports them in their homework, but she is also there to offer counsel, provide advice, and to serve as their surrogate mother, hence her name.

After Ama La shared her story with us, I thanked her and said, "I am moved by your dedication to these young girls. Your hard work, tenacity, and selflessness are an inspiration."

Ama La sat very still and made no acknowledgement. I leaned over and whispered to Kailash, "Does she understand me?"

"She does," he replied.

And so, I continued. "I know you have committed your life to the school and to these girls in your care, but I know it hasn't been easy. Ama La, I would like to honor you with a gift." And still, she did not respond.

After a brief pause, I asked, "What can I provide for you? Something you want, just one thing, in return for all your hard work. What would it be?"

Ama La turned her head and looked around the room where we were meeting, her eyes scanning the area, thinking. I was so excited to hear her response and to be able to provide this amazing woman with something just for her, to celebrate her.

When she returned her gaze, her eyes met mine and she replied, "I would like a generator so during the winter months, the girls don't have to study for their exams while sharing candles for light. It's a very difficult time for them because the electricity comes and goes."

Her response blew me away. I was at a loss for words; this woman, who was given the choice to have anything she asked for, anything that she could have wanted, chose electricity to provide light for the girls.

I said, "Consider it done," and hugged this incredible woman. That afternoon, I purchased a generator made possible by the donations from numerous people on my Facebook Birthday Campaign that year[11]. With the help from a friend who had joined me on this trip, I carried the 80 pound generator up the stairs to the dorm rooms. The look on Ama La's face was priceless. She was delighted! She started crying, which made me cry, and then a few others around us started to cry. It was such a magical moment. A few days later, we returned to Delhi. After settling in to my room, I decided to head down to the lobby, which was always bustling with activity. As soon as the elevator doors opened, I overheard a hostile and disruptive

---

[11] I would like to express my utmost gratitude to everyone who contributed.

scene. There was shouting and commotion at the counter, and when I looked up, I was shocked to find it was the friend who had helped me carry the generator to the school.

I approached the counter and asked my friend what the issue was.

"They are not referring to me by name," he replied with a serious scowl on his crimson face.

"What do you mean?" I asked sincerely, because I had no idea what he was talking about.

"Ajay, I am a Gold member of this hotel chain—the highest level of honor they offer. That means they are supposed to greet me by name every time I walk into the hotel. And not once have they called me by my name or treated me with the kind of respect I deserve."

I was frozen in disbelief. I was trying to process the scene in front of me, but it took a minute to register. We had spent the last couple of days with a woman who lives her life in absolute service of others, someone who never puts anyone else's needs before her own. And, when given the chance to ask for something just for her, she requested an item that would serve the community as a whole.

The hotel where we were staying was modest by American standards, but one where many people on the staff could not afford to stay. Knowing this information reinforced my feelings of gratitude, especially after spending a week in the village with Kailash and Ama La. As a show of appreciation, I had paid for my friend's room, and so it was my name on the register. Although I pointed out this fact, my friend still continued to rant.

"They should know who I am, and greet me with the respect a man of my position is entitled to," he responded, and then walked to the elevators, leaving me to smooth things over with the desk clerk.

The incident at the hotel reinforced the contrast between my friend and Ama La, and reminded me of the reasons I had come to India. He had a sense of entitlement and feelings of superiority, whereas Ama La had a sense of community and feelings of togetherness. He had expectations, where as Ama La had appreciation.

The experience with Ama La showed her selfless nature, a reminder that it's inside all of us—we just have to seek it. So, keep building the muscle of gratitude. The generator she requested brought light to the girls during the winter. How many of us take turning on the lights for granted? I know I do!

If you can be genuinely grateful for something like light, then your appreciation for life and the world changes. When you have more appreciation for life, you will lead a richer and beautiful life. Trade your expectations for appreciations, and your whole life changes.

Gratitude is a surrender, and the expression is unconditional. So how do you know you're truly grateful? When that surrender is authentic, you don't want anything in return.

As soon as you start to feel unappreciated, undervalued, misunderstood, anxious, afraid…STOP! Then find something—running water, the food in your fridge, the phone you casually toss on your bed, your hands, the eyes you're using to read this, and ask yourself what would your life be like without it? What if you had to walk a mile to get a bucket of water? And what if that bucket of water wasn't even for you? What if your eyes stopped working? Once you realize the depths of your fortune, you will start to realize you have an infinite number of things to be grateful for. If you focus on what's not there, you'll miss the beauty of what is there.

I encourage you to truly appreciate life itself and not take it for granted. Be grateful for waking up! As long as you're awake and alive you're grateful.

Students gather for morning meditation.

Ama-La and some of her girls enjoying a beautiful day

Kailash, Ama-La, and me. Pure joy.

Passing out sweets to the children…

Followed by toothbrushes!

Even the staff members were grateful to receive their gifts.

At the end of such a beautiful experience.

Chapter 4:

Be Present to the Present

When I was living in Chicago, I conducted most of my workshops and talks coaching executives in Fortune 500 businesses and other high-powered adults in the city. For the most part, the men and women I worked with were highly educated power brokers, typical titans of their respective industries, who expected preferential treatment. While they were always respectful and considerate during my workshops, I never got the feeling that I was making a huge difference in their lives.

One day, my assistant called me with an opportunity to speak at a Boys and Girls Club in suburb of Milwaukee about an hour's drive from Chicago. While I wasn't familiar with the Boys and Girls Club of America, I knew that the town was a working- class city with a high school completion rate lower than the national average and many of its citizens on public assistance. I immediately agreed to it because I recognized the opportunity to give back and to connect with an underserved community.

I researched the Boys and Girls Club of America and discovered that their mission is to:

Enable all young people, especially those

who need us the most, to reach their full potential

as productive, caring, responsible citizens.

After reading that statement, I was even more excited to speak with the young people in the town in the hopes of contributing something of value to help them realize this mission. They provide a safe environment that fosters hope and focuses on the connection between character and success. Perfect!

On the Saturday morning I was scheduled to speak, I was nervous. I started coming up with all the reasons why I wouldn't connect with the kids - they would think I was too corporate, or that I was too old, or that they wouldn't understand my accent. The more I focused on me, on what I thought was missing, on how the talk would affect me and my reputation, the more anxious I felt. After about 10 minutes of this spiral, I asked myself what could I do right now to change the way I feel? What could I do right now to feel inspired to reach the kids who were waiting for me? They deserved me to show up as my best self. So, I launched into my gratitude exercise and realized how fortunate I was. Immediately, the nervousness became excitement, and I cranked up my music to celebrate! Listening to my favorite songs allowed me to focus on the present moment; I sang along at the top of my lungs, and because I fully committed to the present through the music that I love, all the pain and suffering disappeared. Fear can show up at any time — making a phone call to a potential client, reaching out to a family member or friend you have a strained relationship with, having to take a test or exam, preparing for a job interview — the list can be endless! But the solution is the same. Focus on the truth and the moment; find a way to feel and express gratitude and joy.

It's such a simple act that anyone can do at any moment, and I encourage you to practice this muscle.

When I arrived, I saw kids running around everywhere. Some of the older kids were blasting music from boom boxes, dancing and singing. It reminded me of the party in my car that I had created with my music, and it made me feel even more excited for what the day held.

As soon as I got out of my car, I was immediately approached by the Program Director, who greeted my with a huge smile. I knew it was going to be great! She escorted me to the multi purpose room where there were about 75 kids ranging from 12 - 18 years old. Some of them were running around, chasing each other, yelling and teasing. Many of them had huge smiles on their faces, but there were others who looked angry and frustrated, like they didn't want to be there. I noticed similar reactions from the teachers, staff, and security. This assembly was scheduled at the last minute and interfered with their free time. I refused to allow anything or anyone to disrupt my heightened state, and I recalled the conversation I had with the program director the day before.

"Ajay, these kids are unlike any other ones that you may have spoken to in the past. Some come from very, very disturbed homes. Some are orphans, some have parents in jail, some are always in and out of rehab. You get the picture?"

I made the decision to put all my worries aside and focus on the kids in the room. They needed me, and I would be there 100% for each of them. I only had 45 minutes, and I would do everything I could to plant these seeds. I was excited to serve and give my talk.

At 11:00 am, the program director introduced me as a top speaker from Anthony Robbins, someone who speaks to Fortune 500 companies and top executives throughout the US. I had specifically asked them not to introduce me like this because I didn't want to create any distance between me and the kids; I wanted to be introduced as a friend who loves to help. Her introduction of me was intended to give me authority, but I could see it turned off some of the kids, and some of the adults, as well.

I started my talk and for the first five minutes, I got very little in terms of responses and interaction. Kids were walking around in the back, some were talking loudly, some were even on their phones. It was pretty chaotic so I knew I had to do something to get their attention.

I decided to ask questions to build rapport with the group. As they started engaging, more and more kids started to settle down. That's when I asked, "What is the difference that makes the difference in human beings?"

Silence. Then someone said "What does that even mean?" And everyone started to laugh, including me.

"Let me give you an example," I said. "Why is it that you have two athletes who play the same game on the same team, but only one consistently outperforms everyone on the court?"

"Maybe he got the latest Air Jordan's," boomed a voice from the crowd, causing bursts of laughter.

"I agree. Those shoes are great," I replied. "But if that's all it takes, then every single person with those shoes would excel. So, what else could it be?"

No one offered another reason, and so I continued. "Why do some people workout every day and have tons of energy, but other people always say they don't have the time and put off doing things until next week? Have you ever known someone who has suffered a lot, either they lost their job, or they lost a family member, or got really sick, or even a disaster left them with nothing? These things happen all the time, but one person will just give up and put the blame on anything they can find around. They'll point fingers and be angry and come up with excuses and all the reasons why life is so unfair to them. The same disaster can happen to another person but they will find a way to appreciate the situation, to come up with a solution and take action to turn it all around. Which of these two people would you like to spend time with? The person who's bitter and pissed off and complains all the time? Or the person who realizes they're in control of their life and that there is always a solution, and so they just do whatever it takes to succeed?"

Most of the noise had died down, and the kids were really paying attention here. I knew this idea resonated with them. "What stops people from achieving what they want in life? What stops you from doing whatever you need to succeed?" "I don't have enough time," shouted one kid.

"I got no money," said another.

"How many of you think you need money to make money?" I asked, and half the audience raised their hands. "OK, what else?" "I gotta take care of my brothers and sisters every day after school"

"You need a good education."

"Drugs. Well, not me, but other people."

Then someone said, "Bullies."

I stopped and asked, "Who said 'bullies?'"

A 12-year-old girl raised her hand just slightly, looking shy and timid sitting with other kids her age but who were much bigger than she. I said to her, "That's a great answer, my dear. How many of you in this room also have a problem with bullying or bullies?" Half of the room raised their hands.

"You see? You are not alone, my dear. Everyone gets bullied one way or another."

"Have you ever been bullied?" she asked.

"Yes, many times throughout my life."

"Like, how?" Her voice was small and I realized it must have taken her a great deal of courage to continue this conversation. "When I lived in London, I was bullied quite often. I was called horrible names and made fun of for being overweight and chubby. I was also bullied for the color of my skin. I was physically bullied in elementary school and again in high school after moving to the States. In high school, it was so bad that I had to actually plan my route each day and avoid walking down certain hallways on certain days. I knew that if I ran into the bullies they would attack me. Other days I wouldn't take the bus to school because they were waiting for me, ready for a fight."

She raised her hand again, and I smiled to encourage her to speak. She said, "Have you ever thought about taking your own life?"

There was immediate pin-drop silence in the room. The boys in the back who were messing around stopped and listened. "Yes," I answered. "I've had thoughts like that in the past, but I've never taken any action."

She nodded and her eyes fell to the ground.

"Have you ever thought about taking your own life?" I asked. She replied, "Yes."

I walked so I was in front of where she was standing. "Why did you want to kill yourself?"

She started looking around the room, but I brought her back to look only at me. "Don't worry about anyone else in this room. This is about you and me."

She mentioned emotional abuse from people at school and even from her family.

I pushed her for details. "When you say 'emotional abuse,' what are you talking about specifically?"

"My mom, she isn't always able to take care of me," she said with obvious pain in her voice. "Sometimes I go to stay with my aunt or I sleep over at a friend's. I don't want to be a bother, so I don't get to shower every day. Kids make fun of how bad I smell. They pretend to die or throw up from the smell when I walk by."

She paused, and I encouraged her to continue. "Go on." That's when she really opened up and spoke about the struggles in her life. Her mom was an addict and the cycle was that she would start to get clean but she always slipped back into using. Most days during the week, this girl's only meal came from the one provided for her in school. Her mom never gets her school supplies so she uses items donated by a local insurance company. Everything has their name printed on it so kids at school call her "Geico."

I couldn't believe everything she had gone through in her short life.

"So what do you think it means that there isn't enough food at home? Or that you don't even have a home?"

"I don't matter. Nobody cares about me."

"Nobody?" I pressed.

"My mom doesn't care about me. She picks drugs over me." "And if she doesn't care about you, what else does that mean?" "She's my mom. She's supposed to care."

"You're right. She is, but she doesn't. So what does that mean?" "I just think, if my mom doesn't love me, who else will?" "And so if you don't matter and you're not worthy of love, what's the next thing you think about?"

"No one would miss me if I died."

She paused and I could tell there was something more she wanted to share, so I waited.

"I don't just think about it. I've tried numerous times, but I've failed."

"And why do you think that is?"

"What do you mean?" she asked.

"Why haven't you succeeded in taking your own life?" The whole room went silent again. I could see the looks of horror on the teachers' faces when I asked this question. The program director was shocked, but I knew what I was doing. I felt an energy from this beautiful little girl.

"I don't know."

"Sure you do. Why are you still here? What has kept you from killing yourself?"

She began to cry and melted. "Maybe I am good enough." "*Maybe* you're good enough?" I pressed her further. "What's something you're great at doing? It could be anything." She calmed down and replied, "I'm a pretty good artist." "No you're not!" a boy sitting close to her yelled. I was concerned about this interruption and thought about asking him to leave when he continued. "You're an AMAZING artist!" That's when the crowd broke out into laughter and applause. "And what can you do with your AMAZING artistic talent?" I asked.

"I don't know," she answered almost immediately.

"That's OK. If you did know, what would it be?"

She paused, dropped her eyes, and fidgeted with the zipper on her jacket. "Maybe…I can work with little kids? Teach them about art?"

"Is this something you have done in the past?"

"This doesn't count, but there was this girl here, and I showed her how she could use colors to make herself feel better." "Of course it counts!" I exclaimed. At that moment, her classmates went crazy! They bursted into cheers, dancing and chanting her name. She was shocked at first, but then lit up like a Christmas tree. Her posture and physiology immediately changed, and she started dancing with her friends.

After a few minutes, the celebration settled down and I turned the focus back to her. "When you worked with that girl, how did it make you feel?"

With confidence she replied "It made me feel important because I was able to help someone else."

"That's right. You can share your gift with others, and that way, you will make their lives better. You have this gift and a light inside of you that you need to share! It's not about you, my dear. It's about the difference you can make in other people's lives."

When things calmed down a little, I looked her in the eyes and asked her the question again. "Now, will you ever consider taking your life again?"

Without hesitation she replied "Absolutely not."

"And why not?"

"Because I am here for a reason," she beamed. "I am here to make a difference."

"You are. And there will be times when you doubt yourself. We all do! There will be moments of fear and uncertainty, when you tell yourself you're not good enough. Believe it or not, I have those moments, as well."

Her eyes grew wide and she asked "You do?"

"Yes, but then I remind myself that it's not about me, it's about being of service to others. It's not about what's missing from my life, it's about being grateful for what I do have."

Within minutes, this girl went from thinking about taking her life to knowing that she has value, and that she is here to make a difference on this planet. My friends, if you stop focusing on yourself and focus on the difference you can make to others around you, then your life will be filled with beauty, joy, love, care and above all else, meaning.

When human beings feel loved, acknowledged, and worthy, we lead lives of fulfillment because we see things from a more beautiful perspective. Focus on your light, your gift, your power, your love. Show up as your best self, treat people with kindness and respect - even those who you think don't deserve it, because they are the ones who need it the most.

Sometimes all it takes is being present with someone to understand and help them. One of the reasons why this young girl wanted to end her life—the most common reason why people want to end their lives—is because she believed the lie that she was not good enough. Sadly, no one took the time to let her know how much she matters. That loneliness caused her more pain than she thought she could bear. She believed the only way to end the pain and suffering was to end her life. But all she needed was to be loved unconditionally, to experience genuine interaction, and to be recognized as the precious soul she is.

I followed up with this young girl a couple of months later and learned that she was working with upper management in the organization, guiding other kids in the club who were experiencing something similar to what she had experienced. Now she is the one listening, being present, and offering love and support. She changed the focus from *I* to *We*, and went from *Illness* to *Wellness*!

Chapter 5:

Do the Right Thing

My family and I organized a 10-day, all-inclusive trip where we had the amazing opportunity to meet His Holiness the Dalai Lama (HHDL). The trip began and ended in Delhi for the nine people who came from all corners of the Earth: UK, Netherlands, USA, Malaysia, India, and Kenya. I was ecstatic to know I was finally going to meet HHDL!

After spending four nights in Dharamshala, the home of HHDL, we traveled to Rishikesh to spend four days coaching, mentoring, and teaching children before heading back to Delhi. On the final night of our trip, we hosted a private dinner to celebrate the incredible experience. At the end of the meal, we were feeling so full of joy that we all decided to continue the celebration at one of the most popular Jazz Clubs in Delhi that just happens to be owned by one of my cousins! And on that particular night, a very famous musician was performing. It would be the perfect way to finish this magical trip — spending quality time with the people we love while listening to jazz music.

The hotel arranged for a car to take my parents and some of the people who joined us on this trip to the club while I called for an Uber. It is widely known that transport is inexpensive in India, and that Uber is the easiest way to get around, not to mention the most convenient since most of the drivers do not speak English. Soon after my parents jumped in the hotel car with their friends, I received a notification that the Uber driver was at the hotel, dropping off his last passengers. Looking around, I spotted the Uber driver parked on the side entrance where two men were exiting the car, so my two friends and I headed that way. As we approached, we noticed the driver and the gentlemen being dropped off were exchanging words, as if they were having an argument or misunderstanding. Meanwhile, I was feeling joyful and happy as we'd just experienced a life-changing event, and I was looking forward to joining my parents and other friends to continue the celebration.

I approached the driver and asked, "What's going on? Can we go?"

The driver replied, "Sir, the gentleman refuses to pay me the 200 rupee tip."

"Why are you asking for a 200 rupee[12] tip?" I asked curiously. "Sir," the driver replied with emotion and exhaustion, "I have driven this gentleman all day starting at 9:00am, so it has almost been 12 hours. At the start of the day, he agreed that he would give me an

---

[12] Approximately $3 or €2

additional 200 rupees for my time. All I am asking for is that he honor his word and pay me the 200 rupees, sir." "Bhaiya[13]," I said to put his mind at ease, "I will speak to the passengers and figure this out for you. But please, don't worry! Whatever happens, I will take care of you. Just start my Uber fare and we will leave shortly."

Since there are always two sides of every story, I didn't want to assume I knew the whole picture. I approached the heavy-set, well-dressed European gentleman as he was checking into the hotel and politely asked asked what had happened. I was shocked at his reply.

"I don't want to give the kid a tip. It's his job to drive people around."

I said, "Excuse me, but I just want to clarify the situation because I don't want to get upset over something that may not be right."

The gentleman exhaled audibly and turned back to the hotel clerk.

Not allowing his irritation to deter me, I continued. "The driver informed me that he has been driving you and your friend since 9:00 this morning. He has taken you all around the city and you are only now returning to this hotel, where the average night costs around $300. Yet, you refuse to give this man an extra couple of dollars for the entire day's work?"

---

[13] Brother in Hindi, a sign of respect and camaraderie

He stood his ground and replied, "Yes, that is correct. I am not paying him anything more. He doesn't deserve it." The other man who had accompanied the gentleman I spoke to looked humiliated and embarrassed, as if it wasn't the first time he had witnessed this gentleman treating someone with such disrespect.

"But he said that you agreed to the 200 rupee tip this morning." The man actually scoffed. "I just said that to make sure he wouldn't leave us somewhere during the day."

I was blown away by his arrogance. I said, "You, sir, are selfish, ungrateful, and you have no respect for others. You are paying more than $300 a night for a hotel, but refuse to honor your word and give that hard-working man $3. One day, I hope you find an ounce of gratitude and humility in your heart. Sometimes in life, a small thank you can go along way."

The two clerks behind the check-in desk and the duty manager overheard my comments and out of the corner of my eye,

I saw smiles come from their eyes. It was clear to me that they had seen too many instances like this.

Before I left the hotel to get into the car waiting outside, I said, "I will take care of his tip. I wish you an amazing stay, and I do hope you never treat another human being like that again."

Standing up for that driver was the right thing to do. We have to treat each other with respect and dignity. We have no idea what people are going through and what they have to do to earn enough money to afford food and water.

When I got back to the car, music was playing on the radio and my two friends were sitting in the back seats ready to go. The driver hopped out of his seat to open the door for me.

I put my hand on his shoulder, looked him in the eye, and said, "Bhaiya, thank you for not getting upset or angry. It shows you have true character. And please don't worry about that guy. I will pay you your 200 rupees, so please let's drive." I gave him the name of the club and we were off.

It was only a 10-minute drive, but we blasted some great music and had a lot of fun. The driver was quite serious, but he loosened up a little bit during the journey, which was great to see.

When we reached the club, we all got out of the car. I thanked him for taking us and I handed him a 2000 rupee note. I said, "Bhaiya, this is for you. Enjoy it, and thank you for everything you do." I wasn't expecting anything in return, so I walked off as soon as he took the note.

Before entering the club, I watched him from a distance. For a solid 60-90 seconds, he just stared at that note. Perhaps he had never received such a large note before; maybe he was shocked that someone gave him a week's wages as a tip. That night, it melted my heart to see a young man work all day, but not raise his voice or get upset when things didn't go in his favor. He showed character, discipline, and hard work.

My friends, in life, you will be rewarded for doing the right thing, for standing up for yourself, and for standing up for others. It may not show immediately, but if you consistently stay true to who you are and what you stand for, continue serving others at the highest level without expecting anything in return, the universe will reward you. Just wait and it will happen.

It's important to spread love and light wherever you go and to step in when the time is right to speak your truth. Some people need to be reminded of how beautiful and valuable each person's life is.

Chapter 6

Leading By Example

Tony Robbins tells a now-famous story about an experience when he was 11 years old that taught him one of the most valuable lessons of his life. He witnessed his father reject a huge box of food on Thanksgiving, even though his family was poor and they didn't have much food. His father actually yelled at the man, claiming "We don't take charity!" before slamming the door in his face. His father's reaction came from a place of such shame that he was willing to put his family at harm rather than accept the gift. From that experience, Tony realized that we all have control over three things:

1. What we Focus on

2. What we make it mean, and

3. What we do about it.

Tony was able to get the food, which helped to inspire his commitment to service above self. Through the Anthony Robbins

Foundation, he created the *Basket Brigade*, which feeds millions of families during Thanksgiving.

I want to take a moment to acknowledge Tony Robbins for everything he has done for me and my family. He has guided us and allowed us to experience more of this beautiful thing we call life. Thank you, Brother.

In 1999 when I was eight and my sister was six, my family participated in our first Basket Brigade while we were living in London. It was so powerful to work as a family in this way, and that shared experience reinforced the joy of giving and serving others. Five years later, my sister and I created our first baskets together. That first time, I remember feeling rather grown up since I was taking the lead and doing something meaningful on my own. It became a ritual for us, and something we both really looked forward to. Every year would discuss which items to include, make a list, go shopping, assemble the baskets, and deliver them to people in need in our community. Creating baskets is still one of my favorite things to do as we continued the practice after moving to the states. In fact, it's so engrained in my life that I was able to introduce it to some friends while on a trip to Kansas in early 2022.

Thanks to the vision I share with my dear friend Tony W., I had the opportunity to spend an inspired weekend in Lawrence, Kansas. Now, for those NCAA fans reading this, you'll recognize that town as the home of the National Champion Jayhawks. In January 2022, Tony was able to secure a recording studio on the KU campus where

I spent over 12 hours recording my life story, including some stories from this book, as well as the tools and strategies I've learned along the way.

Tony is the father of three boys, and his youngest son, Alexander[14], got permission to spend Friday with us in the studio. We made it worthwhile for Alexander, who was 11 years old at the time, so he could see the value in our project and realize that learning takes place everywhere - not just in school. Alexander is full of energy, life, and, mostly love, which makes him such an awesome kid to be around! One of the lessons for the day was "The Secret to Living is Giving," and Tony and I decided to create an experience that Alexander would never forget. As I mentioned earlier, Tony and I share a similar outlook on life; it's all about experiences, and the more we can create for ourselves and the people we love, the more of life we will enjoy and remember. So, Tony and I worked out a plan to show Alexander, rather than simply tell him, what "The Secret to Living is Giving" really means. After we finished recording for the day, we took Alexander to a local homeless camp where about 12 people had set up tents. "We don't have anything to give them," Alexander said as we got out of the car.

"That's because we don't know what they need," Tony replied. "We could guess, but Ajay and I think it's better to ask them instead of just assuming we know what's best for them."

---

[14] His name has been changed to protect his identity.

I could see the wheels turning in Alexander's brain. He probably had never thought about giving in this way before now. But was he in for a life-changing experience!

As expected, they asked for food, water, and some personal hygiene items, but one of the men asked for a propane tank so they could stay warm in the 35 degree weather.

"I never would have thought of that," said Alexander as we climbed back into the car. He was really quiet on the drive to the store, which was rare for this energetic and talkative kid.

When we arrived at the store, we gave Alexander a budget of $100 and told him it was his responsibility to select food for the 12 people. He was so excited to be given an opportunity to help, and he walked around the store with the calculator out on his phone to tally up the costs. He did such a great job of selecting mostly nutritious items, plus some treats and snacks.

Once we check out of the store, we brought everything to the back of Tony's SUV. Together, the three of us made 12 bags of essentials, including food and water, a toothbrush, and other items. Tony didn't start the car, so we were freezing while packing the bags. We then got back in the car and headed back to the camp site.

"We were only outside for like 10 minutes and I can't feel my fingertips," Alexander said while looking out the window. "I can't imagine what it would be like to be outside all day and night."

Out of the corner of my eye, I could see a smile creep onto Tony's face as he drove. Alexander gave him so many reasons to be proud.

When we reached the camp site, everyone was so happy and appreciative for the gifts. Alexander's face beamed as he handed out each individual a bag of supplies, bragging that he chose the items to include. Then, Tony and I pulled two propane tanks from his SUV and helped them set it up to generate some heat. We said goodbye, got back into the car, and headed home.

"So, Alexander. I'm curious," I said after a few minutes. "What did you learn from this experience?"

"I learned that it's important to ask people how you can help them, because I never would have thought of a propane tank!" "Neither did we, son!" said Tony. "That was something I learned today, too."

"I was so surprised at how good it felt giving those bags to all those people in the park," Alexander continued. "In that moment, I felt really happy."

"Anything else?" I asked after a minute.

"I didn't realize that a kid my age could make a difference." We rode the rest of the way home listening to some music, Alexander singing from the back seat.

When we arrived home, Alexander ran into the house. I looked at Tony and asked "Xbox?"

"I don't know. Maybe."

But when we walked in the door, we could hear Alexander telling his mom, Jen, about his day at the studio and then about the experience at the camp site. She was beaming as her son recounted every detail. When he finished, he ran into the kitchen and after a minute he called out "Anyone else hungry?"

From time to time, I would send Alexander a text and let him know I was thinking about him. He always replied with something positive and upbeat. Then, on April 3, 2022, Tony called me and said, "You will never guess what happened." I could hear the smile in his voice.

The night before, Alexander and Jen went to a local entertainment spot with a bowling alley, an arcade, and every TV airing the NCAA Final Four game between Kansas and Villanova. Jen met up with some friends and colleagues, and Alexander's best friend, Marcus[15], was there, as well.

Alexander is a HUGE basketball fan, and an even bigger Jayhawks fan. He really knows his stuff, so it was no surprise that he won a $60 bet with some of his mom's friends. Alexander handed Marcus $20 and then put the remaining cash into his wallet.

---

[15] His name has been changed to protect his identity.

"What's this for?" asked Marcus with a confused look. "Whatever you want!" replied Alexander.

They watched the rest of the game as Kansas beat Villanova and then Alexander, Marcus, and Jen headed downtown to meet up with Tony (and the rest of Lawrence!) to celebrate KU's victory. The Jayhawks would be playing for the national championship Monday night!

As was expected, downtown was packed, and there were thousands of people celebrating in the streets. Tony had arrived and made his way through the crowd when he saw Alexander and Marcus. He called to them, but they didn't hear him because they were talking with a woman who was wrapped up in layers of clothes standing by a shopping cart. Now here's where the magic happened, and it didn't have anything to do with NCAA basketball. Tony watched as his son give the woman $20 from his wallet. She thanked him, and Alexander and Marcus started to walk away. Tony was blown away by his son's generosity! He started to call his name again, but then Marcus stopped walking, said something to Alexander, and they headed back to where the woman was sitting. Marcus took the $20 bill that Alexander had given him and handed it to the woman. Clearly, Alexander had taught Marcus the most important lesson in life: true happiness comes from giving. When we give from a place of pure love and without expecting anything in return, we find peace and joy.

Later that evening when they got home, Tony went into Alexander's room as he was getting ready for bed.

"Did you have fun tonight?" asked Tony.

"It was the best day of my life! The Jayhawks are going to the National Championship, and I won $60 in a bet!"

"I saw what you did, Alexander," Tony said, sitting on the edge of his son's bed.

"What did I do?" asked Alexander nervously.

Tony smiled and gave a little laugh. "No, son. Nothing like that. I saw you give money to that woman."

"Oh!" Alexander's smile beamed. "You saw that?"

Tony nodded his head.

"She really needed help," Alexander continued.

"Yeah. She looked like she did. I'm really proud of you, son." "Thanks, dad." Alexander paused, reflecting on the moment. "But do you know who I'm really proud of? Marcus. I gave the lady half of my money, but Marcus gave her everything he had." Tony just listened as his son shared his thoughts. "Look, you know I'm getting really good at this giving unconditionally stuff, but

Marcus, well, this is all new to him. He told me he gave that lady $20 because he saw me give her $20. Pretty cool, huh?" Tony smiled and nodded his head. "Pretty cool."

What's amazing about that story of Alexander and Marcus is that, if Tony hadn't witnessed it, he wouldn't have known it happened. Alexander and Marcus never shared it with anyone. They gave unconditionally — they didn't even want recognition for it.

While Alexander is a remarkable kid in so many ways, he is also just like every other 10 year old kid. I think this experience serves to show how important it is to introduce children to small acts of kindness, like making the bags for the people at the homeless camp. There are so many opportunities to teach them how to express gratitude, giving, compassion, and love. And each activity or experience that parents and other family members do with their children will give them a sense of community and belonging that will connect them to humanity in profound ways.

Chapter 7:

The Dadaji Method™

We have talked a lot about the importance of giving unconditionally and expressing gratitude, of living from a place of love and kindness, and most of the stories in this book have been about service to others. But there is something just as important, and that is showing kindness, love, and gratitude to ourselves. We have the privilege of being alive and the gift hands, eyes, feet, a sense of humor, the ability to feel all the emotions and use our incredible brains. But how many of us realize what this gift really means and how lucky we are to be alive? In fact, researchers have determined that the human body is worth on average $6 million! That's more than most people will earn in a lifetime. Knowing that you are worth MILLIONS of dollars, what changes would you make? What would you do to make sure you safeguard that precious gift? It's easy to take things for granted—we all do it—and sometimes, it takes a global lockdown and threats to our entitlement for us to make changes and start to honor ourselves as precious.

After a series of unplanned events, I flew to London for a family event in March 2020. A few days before I was scheduled to return to India, the British government mandated a strictly enforced lock-down and people were not permitted to leave the house, much less the country. Since I was a US citizen, I had the option to fly to Orlando, but I decided to remain in the UK and live with Dadaji[16], my then 89-year-old grandfather. At the time, I had no idea how much Dadaji and I would learn from each other over the next 15 months.

My grandfather has always been someone I admire and look up to, and, until circumstances forced a roommate on him, he had lived alone since 1998. He had a solid daily routine filled with rituals, activities, and self-care practices. He took daily walks, held a plank for at least a minute, practiced yoga, juiced daily, cooked his own meals, prayed and honored his late wife twice a day. In addition, he went to Windsor Leisure Centre, the gym where he had held a membership for almost 60 years, and swam and lifted weights at least three times a week. He maintained an active social life with friends he had known since arriving in the UK in 1965. All of this was remarkable for an 89-year-old man. But what made it even more incredible was the fact that he committed to his daily routine despite having COPD (Chronic Obstructive Pulmonary Disease), Triple Heart Bypass, Double Pacemaker, Volvulus, and Age-Related Macular Degeneration.

---

[16] "Grandfather" in Hindi

Understandably, when COVID-19 threatened the world, it was in the best interest for Dadaji's physical health to remain indoors. He was, after all, a very high-risk candidate. However, we never considered the impact that the isolation would have on Dadaji's well-being. Ironically, the thing that was keeping him alive was also slowly killing him. For the next 14 weeks, this active, vibrant, curious, social man never left the house. His life came to a screeching halt and not once did he ever complain. He continued to practice what he could from the confines of the house, but the lack of aerobic exercise, social connections, and fresh air took its toll and his health started to seriously deteriorate. The first week of July, he suffered a mini- heart attack. We were faced with a dilemma: either go to the doctor and risk exposure to COVID, or stay and watch him continue to decline.

In July 2020, I was 29 years old. I had been practicing the muscles of gratitude, mindset, and focus for two-thirds of my life! However, the circumstances of being fully responsible for my grandfather caused me to question everything I had practiced. It was one thing for me to make decisions and choices for myself, but now I was faced with having to make decisions and choices not only for someone else's life, but for the life of a man whom I had grown up admiring, respecting, and loving, and I couldn't afford to make any "wrong" decisions. I noticed I would feel anxious each time I thought about what to do for my grandfather. That was when I decided that fear was not going to rule my actions. Coming from a place of certainty, confidence, and perseverance would eliminate all sense of doubt, apprehension, and anxiety. Every experience in my life and every muscle I had developed — patience, love, communication, kindness — had prepared me for this challenge. I knew it would all come down to mindset.

In anticipation of having a serious conversation with him, I reflected on my time with Dadaji and realized something seemingly insignificant that inspired me. It dawned on me that whenever things would break around the house, let's say there was an issue with the kitchen faucet and disposal, my immediate reaction was to call a plumber or repairman. But my grandfather would go to a cabinet or a drawer, pull out a few items, and fix it. This man was so resourceful and self-reliant! He lived his life solving problems, and that mindset would translate to his health.

Together, we decided to focus on solutions instead of the problem. Yes, COVID-19 was a potential threat, but it was nothing compared to the despair and sadness I started to witness in my grandfather. So, we started to take walks outside to get more fresh air. We put notes around the house to remind ourselves to drink more water. We totally focused on healing, and we made the shift together.

We focused on seeing the best doctors and specialists; not settling for one way or one opinion. We committed to finding approaches and techniques that worked for him, even if that meant driving an hour each way and paying a little extra out of pocket. Maintaining this commitment was not easy and we were constantly defending our decision because people in the UK receive universal healthcare. Each time we had an appointment in London, his friends and family members challenged him, asking why he was paying for a doctor in London if he was getting it for free down the street? Everyone told him just to use the local doctors. Every week, it was a battle to combat the conflicting belief systems of people he knew and trusted. But our resolve was unshakeable and my grandfather showed me that it's never too late to embrace change and to let go of fear, especially since his "why" was so strong!

During this time of physical healing, I wanted to help my grandfather heal emotionally, as well. There was a period when it seemed like he was attending a "Zoom Funeral" once or twice a week. His lifelong friends were departing this world, and I noticed that he continued to hold onto some resentment toward one particular individual. I broached the subject, but my grandfather dismissed my concerns, saying it wasn't worth discussing. So, I let it go for a while, and then brought it up again. Again, he downplayed the importance of the grudge and asked me to drop it. This went on for a while, me gently introducing the topic, Dadaji waving his hand in the air, almost as if he were erasing it from his consciousness, but each time we had the conversation, I could tell he wasn't dismissing it as easily as he wanted me to believe. However, I could also tell that bringing this up with him was causing him unnecessary stress, which affected his usually happy demeanor. More than that, I know that if I had continued to push the issue, it would have put more pressure on his heart. It was an important discovery for me to accept my grandfather's decision, despite not knowing why he needed to hold onto these feelings. In fact, I recognized that there were people in my life who had hurt me, and whom I had chosen not to forgive. *I told myself, He's doing everything else. He's meeting me at every request. Just let it go. I couldn't, nor did I want to, force him to do anything.* I had to step back and honor his journey.

My time with Dadaji reminded me that everything in life is a choice. Forgiveness is a choice. Seeking revenge is a choice. Happiness is a choice. Suffering is a choice. Whether or not we let go and move on is a choice. How we choose to respond to even the most difficult injustices defines who we are. And when we choose love and when we respond in love, through love, with love, it changes everything.

So…choose love!

To book a Discovery Call with Ajay go to

www.AjayGuptainspires.com/call

Made in the USA
Monee, IL
13 April 2023